SHERLOCK HOLMES'

Fiendish Puzzles

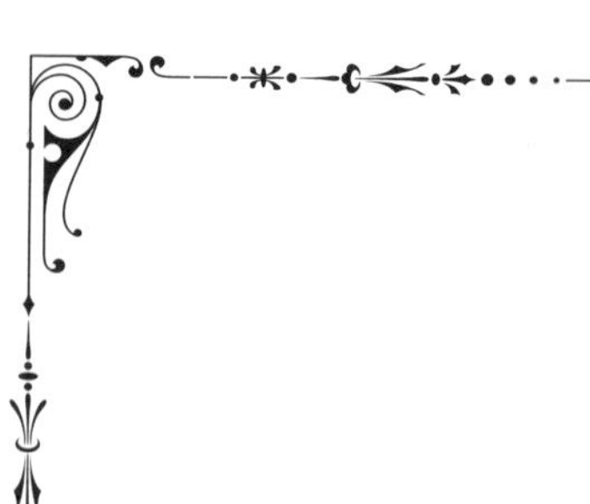

THIS IS A CARLTON BOOK

Published by Carlton Books Ltd
20 Mortimer Street
London W1T 3JW

A CIP catalogue for this book is available from the British Library.

ISBN 978-1-78097-807-9

Text and puzzles: Tim Dedopulos

Full-page original artworks: Rebecca Wright
Additional art: Chris Gould

The publishers would like to thank Mary Evans Picture Library for their kind permission to reproduce the pictures in this book which appear on the following pages:

12, 14, 16, 17, 19, 20, 21, 26-30, 33, 35, 40, 42, 43, 46, 47, 48, 49, 54, 56, 58-61, 66, 67, 73, 74, 78, 79, 80, 81, 82, 84, 88, 91, 96, 98, 101, 102, 104, 105, 106, 108, 112, 114, 115, 118, 121, 122, 126, 130, 132-135, 138, 140,143

Every effort has been made to acknowledge correctly and contact the source and/or copyright holder of each picture and Carlton Books Limited apologises for any unintentional errors or omissions, which will be corrected in future editions of this book.

Content previously published as *The Sherlock Holmes' Puzzle Collection*.

Printed in Dubai

SHERLOCK HOLMES'

Fiendish Puzzles

Riddles, enigmas and challenges inspired by the world's greatest crime-solver

Dr John Watson

CARLTON BOOKS

Contents

Introduction 8

Cunning Puzzles — Question — Answer

Puzzle	Question	Answer
Statuette	14	100
Cold Hands	15	100
Dedication	16	101
Grains of Sand	17	101
The Green Stone	18	102
The First Curiosity	20	102
The Cult of the Red Star	21	103
Afternoon	22	103
Dimples	23	103
Suffocation	24	104
The First Literal Oddity	26	104
The First Mental Trial	27	105
Watch Out	28	105
Afghan Shot	29	106
The Dinner Table	30	106
The Bicycle	31	107
Highland Fling	32	107
Big Squares	34	108

	Question	Answer
The Second Literal Oddity	35	108
The Switch	36	109
The Circus	37	109
The First Portmanteau	38	110
Urchins	40	110
The Meadow of Death	41	111
The Third Literal Oddity	42	111
Gold	43	112
Stones	44	112
Hudsons Tangled	45	113
The Second Curiosity	46	114
Fencing	47	114
The Soho Pit	48	115
The Second Mental Trial	49	115
The Hanged Man	50	116
Happy Family	51	116
The Barn	52	117

Fiendish Puzzles

	Question	Answer
The Third Mental Trial	56	120
In Paris	57	120
Pop Pop	58	121
Evasion	59	122
Six-Sided Dice	60	122
The Fourth Mental Trial	61	123
The Dictionary	62	123
The Third Curiosity	63	124
The Fish Murder	64	124
A Hearty Drop	65	125
The Box	66	126
Sheep	67	126
The Second Portmanteau	68	127
Get A Hat	70	128
Nephews	71	128
The Fifth Mental Trial	72	129
Equity	73	129
Twenty Thousand Leagues	74	130
The Shoreditch Bank	75	130
Markham	76	131

	Question	Answer

Montenegro 78 132
Wordplay 79 132
Wimbledon Common 80 133
The Sixth Mental Trial 81 134
Most Irregular 82 135
Carl Black 83 136
A Matter of Time 84 136
The Faulty Watch 85 137
A Puzzling Portmanteau 86 137
The Ladies of Morden 88 138
A Fascinating Curiosity 89 139
Groups 90 139
The Eggtimer's Companion 91 140
A Curious Mental Trial 92 140
Cones 93 141
Down on the Farm 94 141
Board 95 142
The Night Watchman 96 143
A Literal Oddity 97 143

INTRODUCTION

The name of my dear friend and companion Mr. Sherlock Holmes is familiar to all who possess any interest whatsoever in the field of criminal investigation. Indeed, there are some weeks where it hardly seems possible to pick up a newspaper without seeing his name splashed luridly across the front page. Unlike so many, however, his renown is justly deserved – not for nothing has he frequently been heralded as England's greatest detective, living or dead. Personally, I suspect that his abilities are unmatched anywhere in the world at this time.

I myself have been fortunate enough to share in Holmes' extraordinary adventures, and if I have been unable to rival his insight, I have consoled myself by acting as his de facto chronicler. I also flatter myself a little with the notion that I have, betimes, provided some little warmth of human companionship. We have spent many years, on and off, sharing rooms at 221b Baker Street, and I like to think that the experience has enriched both our existences. My name, though it is of little matter, is John Watson, and I am by profession a doctor.

My dear friend has long had a passionate ambition to improve the minds of humanity. He has often talked about writing a book that will help to instil the habits which he considers so absolutely vital to the art of deduction. Such a tome would be a revolutionary step in the history of mankind, and would most certainly address observation, logical analysis, criminal behaviour, scientific and mathematical knowledge, clear thinking, and much more besides. Alas, it has yet to materialise, for the world is full of villainy, and Sherlock Holmes is ever drawn to the solution of very real problems.

But over the course of our adventures, Holmes has never given up on the cause of improving my modest faculties. On innumerable occasions, he has presented me with opportunities to engage my mind, and solve some problem or other which to him is perfectly clear from the information already available. These trials have sometimes been quite taxing, and have not always come at a welcome moment, but I have engaged in all of them to the very best of my abilities. To do otherwise would be to dishonour the very generous gift my friend is making me in devoting time to my analytical improvement.

In truth, I do believe that his ministrations have indeed helped. I consider myself to be more aware than I was in my youth, and less prone to hasty assessments and faulty conclusions. If I have gained any greater talent in these areas, it is entirely thanks to the efforts that my friend has exerted on my behalf, for it is most certainly not an area for which I am naturally disposed. Give me a sickly patient, and I feel absolutely confident of swiftly arriving at the appropriate diagnosis and, to the limits provided by medical science, of attaining a successful recovery for the poor unfortunate. But my mind does not turn naturally to criminality, violence or deception. If this were a perfect world, then we would all co-exist in genial and honourable honesty, and I would be perfectly suited for the same. Alas, that is far from the case, and my dear friend is far better adapted to the murky undertows of the real world than I.

Still, as I have already attested, Holmes' little trials have had a beneficial effect even on me. For one who is more readily disposed to such efforts, the results may well be commensurately powerful. Thus, I have taken the liberty of assembling this collection.

Working assiduously from my notes, I have compiled somewhere in the region of one hundred and fifty of the puzzles that Holmes has set me over the years. I have been assiduous in ensuring that I have described the situation as I first encountered it, with all pertinent information reproduced. The answers are as detailed as I can usefully make them. Some I managed to answer successfully myself; for others, I have reproduced Holmes' explanations as accurately as my notes permit.

To improve the accessibility a little, I have ordered the trials into two groupings of difficulty – cunning and fiendish. Holmes has a devious mind, and there were times when he was entirely determined to baffle me, whilst on other occasions, the problems were simple enough to serve as illustrative examples of certain principles. I believe that

I have broadly succeeded in classifying the difficulty of his riddles, but I beg your indulgence in so uncertain a matter. Every question is easy, if you know the answer, and the opposite holds equally true.

If is my fervent hope that you will find this little volume enlightening and amusingly diverting. If it may prove to sharpen your deductive sense a little, that would be all the vindication that I could ever possibly wish; all the credit for such improvement would be due Holmes himself. I, as always, am content to be just the scribe. I have taken every effort to ensure that the problems are all amenable to fair solution, but if by some remote happenchance that should prove not the case, it must be clear that the blame lies entirely on my shoulders, and that none should devolve to my dear companion.

My friends, it is with very real pleasure that I present to you this volume of the puzzles of Mr. Sherlock Holmes.

I remain, as always, your servant,

Dr John H. Watson

CUNNING PUZZLES

"My name is Sherlock Holmes.
It is my business to know what
other people don't know."

Sherlock Holmes

THE STATUETTE

Holmes set aside his newspaper and looked up at me over breakfast one morning. "Do you suppose you have a head for business, Watson?"

"I dare say I'd be able to pick it up," I replied.

Holmes tapped the paper thoughtfully. "Let us suppose that you are a seller of antiquities. You have in your possession a rather pleasant statuette. A distinguished elderly gentleman comes in to your premises, and declares that the piece is familiar to him. He purchases it enthusiastically, not even blinking at your £100 price tag.

"Once the transaction is complete, the gentleman informs you that the piece is one of a pair; fairly valued by yourself as a singleton, but worth many times that amount if coupled with its mate. He offers to pay you a massive £1000 if you can obtain the other, and tells you his hotel. He leaves, and naturally you begin making enquiries about the statuette.

"Some days later, a fellow comes by with an identical companion to the statuette you sold. He says that he's heard you're looking for his piece, and is willing to part with it for £300. What say you? Does that sound like a good deal?"

What say you indeed?

SOLUTION ON PAGE 100

Cold Hands

"I have another little thermal question for you," Holmes said to me.

"As you wish," I replied.

"Breathe slowly onto the palm of your hand. Yes, like so. How does it feel?"

"Well," said I, "warm and damp."

"Quite. Now repeat the process, but this time purse your lips and blow vigorously."

"The effect is considerably cooler," I said.

"But your breath – and your hand – are the same temperature on both occasions. So why the difference?"

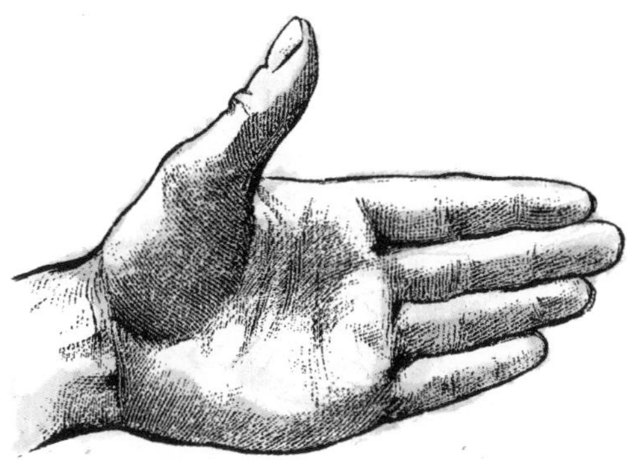

SOLUTION ON PAGE 100

DEDICATION

I took the opportunity, over a luncheon of Mrs. Hudson's fine ham and sliced tomatoes, to take my turn in throwing a little unexpected riddle at Holmes. He was amused, if hardly baffled, so I feel it may be of some entertainment to you.

There is a shop which is devoted to the sale of one particular staple of daily life. It sells many varieties of this particular device, all of which serve exactly the same broad purpose. Some of these varieties are made up of tens of thousands of individual, moving pieces, whilst others consist of less than twenty such parts. A few are completely solid, immobile throughout, and yet still function as well as the most complex. They may likewise range in size from taller and heavier than a man down to being less than the size of a fingernail, but the very tiniest can still have more separate moving parts than the largest.

Can you guess the identity of this device?

SOLUTION ON PAGE 101

GRAINS OF SAND

Holmes, one morning, somewhat startled me by producing an hourglass and waving it under my nose.

"Let's put your deductive mind to work, Watson. This hourglass has run its course. If I turn it over, so that the sand within it is flowing downwards, will it be minutely lighter on account of having some of its constituent parts in weightless free fall?"

I had to think about that for a moment.

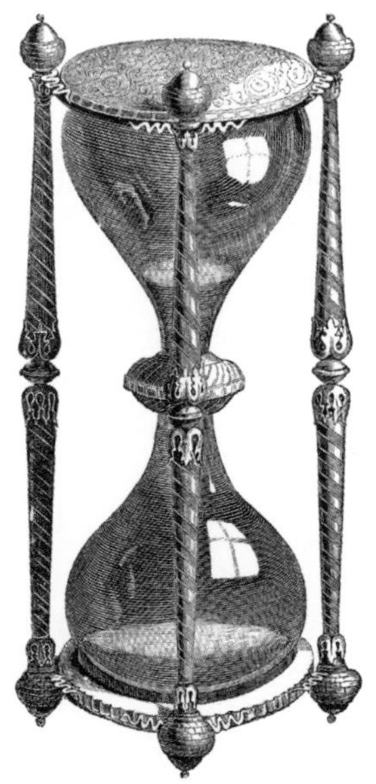

SOLUTION ON PAGE 101

THE GREEN STONE

Holmes and I were pursuing an unfortunate incident connected to the theft of the Green Stone of Harvington. The owners, Rupert and Rebecca Coynes, had come into its possession some years before. On the evening of the theft, the couple had met for refreshments at a London hotel when Rupert had a seizure and collapsed dead. It was later found that he had been poisoned, and mere blind luck had helped Rebecca avoid the same fate.

After the Stone's return, Rebecca had difficulty understanding why she had lived whilst her husband had died. They had both been perfectly healthy and followed a very similar diet. Both their drinks had been laced with identical amounts of toxin, and Rebecca's resilience and constitution was no different to her husband's. To her credit, she refused to believe that it was some divine providence that spared her, but understandably, the matter plagued her with considerable guilt.

Sherlock Holmes bore Rebecca's anguished confusion placidly, and when her tears had subsided, said "Tell me, were you thirsty that evening?" Rebecca nodded, obviously perplexed. Holmes smiled, and said nothing, and it was left to me to explain.

SOLUTION ON PAGE 102

The First Curiosity

"Mrs Hudson informs me that her greengrocer was unable to provide her with her usual 12" bundle of leeks at the market today, and instead gave her two 6" bundles."

"Ah well," I said, my mind not on leeks.

"He had her pay a little extra as well, for the effort involved in making the two bundles."

"Seems reasonable enough," I said. But was it?

SOLUTION ON PAGE 102

THE CULT OF THE RED STAR

Holmes was reading one of his penny dreadfuls. After a short time, be put the pamphlet down and sighed. "It is obvious," said he, "that the murder was committed by the victim's father's brother-in-law. Or the victim's brother's father-in-law. Or, I suppose, the victim's father-in-law's brother. I hate it when the case is so transparent."

It didn't sound in the least bit transparent to me, and I said so. "You yourself cannot even decide between three possible murderers."

"Nonsense," Holmes said crisply. "There is only one possible candidate, and I have identified him precisely."

What did he mean?

SOLUTION ON PAGE 103

AFTERNOON

"Let's keep your mind on its toes," Holmes said to me as I was looking out of the window one afternoon.

I made no protest, so he continued.

"How many minutes are we now before 6pm, if fifty minutes ago it was four times as many minutes past 3pm?"

SOLUTION ON PAGE 103

23

DIMPLES

We were walking in Hyde Park one summery afternoon when I spotted a golf ball under the edge of a bush. I fished it out and had a glance at it.

"Look, Holmes, a guttie. One hardly sees a featherie any more, but they were all the thing in my father's day."

"Someone has been practising his putting," Holmes replied. "A short man, I'd say. But yes, the new balls totally outclass the old. It's not just the rubbery gutta-percha on the inside, however."

"Is it not?"

"You're not a golfing man. The dimples make the ball travel up to four times as far as an identical but undimpled specimen would."

"I've thought of taking it up," I said. "It may help me improve my physical condition. But why would dimples make such a dramatic difference?"

SOLUTION ON PAGE 103

SUFFOCATION

Lady Casterton was found suffocated to death in her bedroom shortly after 7pm, when the maid went to discover why her employer had not appeared for dinner. From an examination of the body, it was clear that she had been killed a little after six at the very earliest. Suspicion naturally fell onto her nephew, her inheritor, with whom relations had been strained in recent weeks. He would have looked like a prime suspect, were it not for the testimony of the maid.

"He left the house at 11 minutes to 6. I'm certain of it. I was in the drawing room, tidying. I heard him leave, clear as anything, and looked up to check the time. He doesn't usually depart before dinner, see? So I looked up at the clock, and thought to myself, 'Why, it's not even 10 to, yet.' So it can't be him. I won't see an innocent man swing."

With no other suspects or evidence of intruders, and the maid's physical weakness ruling her out, the police eventually turned to Baker Street for assistance. Holmes seemed interested briefly, but took a quick look inside the door, then called the maid over and asked her a single question.

Do you understand the situation?

SOLUTION ON PAGE 104

The First Literal Oddity

One afternoon, Holmes handed me a scrap of notepaper. It bore a short list of words, like so:

uncopyrightable
dermatoglyphics
misconjugatedly
hydropneumatics

"One of your word puzzles," I surmised.

"Indeed," said Holmes. "Taken together, these words are the longest English examples of what, exactly?"

SOLUTION ON PAGE 104

The First Mental Trial

We were sitting at breakfast when Holmes said to me, "Let us return to my hypothetical friend for a moment, my dear Watson."

"The wily Alfie."

"Just so. Today, he is joined by several members of his family – Fred, George and Harry. The four were sitting down to tea together, when Alfie noted that George had the same familial relationship to Fred as he himself did to Harry. Furthermore, Alfie himself had the same familial relationship to Fred as George did to him."

"A knotty matter."

"Can you untangle it?"

SOLUTION ON PAGE 105

WATCH OUT

"You know that I have no great love of the Alps," Holmes said. We had been talking idly about skiers. "One of the lesser known perils is that it can be difficult to keep the precise time."

"You mean you get distracted?"

"Not a bit of it," Holmes replied. "Both our pocket watches are scrupulously accurate. If I were to go and spend a period of time up in the Alps, making sure to keep my pocket watch at a healthy room temperature at all times, when I returned here our watches would show a noticeable difference. Despite the fact that the accuracy of my watch should not have suffered one iota from the experience. Can you account for it?"

SOLUTION ON PAGE 105

AFGHAN SHOT

I remember a puzzling problem that I encountered courtesy of a fellow soldier in Afghanistan. He was the quartermaster, and was trying to take consignment of a box of small cannon shot, iron balls precisely two inches across. The crate that he had received was 14" in depth, $24\frac{9}{10}$" in length, and $22\frac{4}{5}$" wide, and it was packed to the brim. Sadly, it neglected to list the number of balls it contained.

Can you deduce how many shot balls were in the crate?

THE ILLUSTRATED LONDON NEWS

SOLUTION ON PAGE

106

THE DINNER TABLE

"My hypothetical friend Alfie is having a dinner party," Holmes informed me.

I prepared my brain as best I could for one of his typically baffling onslaughts.

"In addition to Bill and Charlie, he is also expecting Don, Eric, Fred and George."

"Quite a turn-out," I said.

"Alfie is setting places around a circular table, and wants to ensure everyone gets to sit next to everyone else, so he is having them change places between each of the three courses. He is however a little tired of George, and always fond of Bill. His intention is to arrange everyone around the table in alphabetical order for the starter. How should he arrange the men for the other two courses to ensure everyone sits beside everyone else, yet still keep Bill as close as that will allow, and George as distant?"

SOLUTION ON PAGE 106

THE BICYCLE

One afternoon, at my medical practice, I overheard a young patient attempting to extort a gift of a bicycle from her mother as a reward for the girl's good behaviour in complying with my ministrations. The mother was amused, as was I, but remained resolute.

"You can have a bicycle when you are exactly one third of my age, and not before. You are still too young, and I don't want you haring around on one of those things."

The little girl clearly deemed this acceptable, for she was perfectly sweet throughout her examination. I knew from my notes that she was 13, and her mother was 46. When I put the situation to Holmes, he was able to work out how long it would be before the girl got her bike in a flash.

Can you do so?

SOLUTION ON PAGE

Highland Fling

"Superstitious nonsense!" Sherlock Holmes slammed his newspaper down on the desk in irritation.

I enquired mildly regarding the nature of the story that had aroused my friend's ire.

"It is in the nature of the weak mind to ever seek supernatural intervention in even the simplest of matters," he replied, more calmly. "This article spins a tale of a supposedly Highland marriage, and the supposed curse that has been inflicted upon it. All utter nonsense."

"Of course," said I.

"A young couple chose this Candlemas just past for their nuptials. As the ceremony was progressing, a local girl burst in to the church and declared that as she had been passed over by the groom, she had ensured that the marriage would be a doomed one. As a sign, the church bell would not ring to celebrate their union. She then consumed some poisonous concoction, and staggered back out in a suitably theatrical manner. She was later found dead."

"I say!"

"The ceremony resumed, but the entire wedding party was afflicted with horror when, at the climax, the Church bell did indeed fail to sound. The bride fainted dead away, and several other ladies had to be attended to. When the groom and his man went with the vicar to investigate, they could find no sign of tampering, and indeed the bell worked again thereafter. So, being feeble-witted, they all declared it had to be the work of the devil in league with the spurned witch girl, and the bride has barely eaten nor slept since."

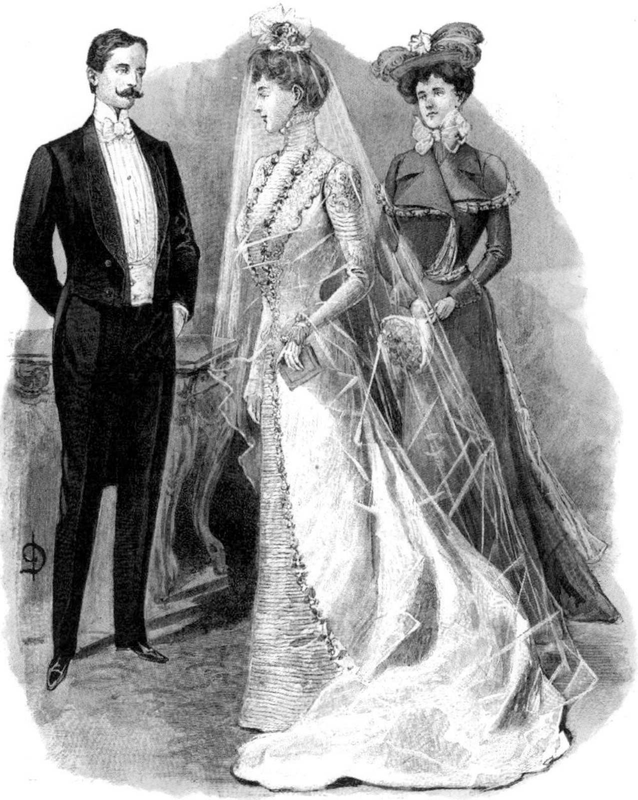

It was clear Holmes had a different explanation in mind. Can you imagine what?

SOLUTION ON PAGE 107

Big Squares

Holmes cornered me near the window, and expressed concern that his previous challenge to me involving the arrangement of each of the nine digits from 1 to 9 into a series of square numbers had not been stern enough.

I tried to persuade him that I felt most mathematically enlightened, but he was most insistent that I try again, this time to combine all of the digits into one single, massive square number. As if such a request were not enough, he casually added that it had to be the smallest possible such square.

I agreed as graciously as possible, and retired to my notepaper.

Can you find the answer?

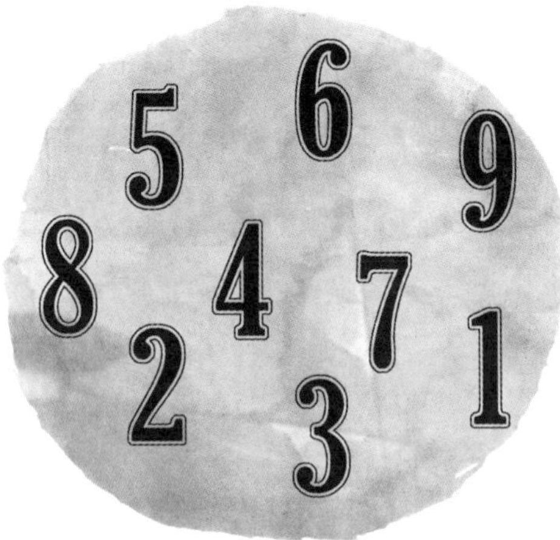

SOLUTION ON PAGE 108

The Second Literal Oddity

"Tell me, Watson," Holmes said. How many words in English use do you think there are that end with the letters -bt?"

"Well," I began, "there must be..."

"Careful man, give it a little thought."

I took his advice, and I'd suggest you do the same.

SOLUTION ON PAGE

THE SWITCH

"Observe the time would you, Watson old chap?"

I did as instructed. "Just a little after 4.42, Holmes."

He nodded. "So when the positions of the hands are exactly reversed, it will be a bit after 8.23."

"Just so," I agreed.

"Given that the position of the hour hand is fixed precisely, moment by moment, by the exact movement of the minute hand, there are only a limited number of times in any given period when the positions of the hands will exactly swap locations. If it was 4.45, there would be no reverse alignment."

"I can see that," I said.

"So how many times do you think the hands of a clock will exactly reverse themselves between 3pm and midnight?"

SOLUTION ON PAGE 109

37

THE CIRCUS

It was a chilly November evening when Holmes informed me that he had obtained tickets to attend a circus on Clapham Common that very night. I expressed a certain amount of surprise, given that he had never shown enthusiasm for such diversions.

"Ah," said he. "I have had word that there may be some foul play afoot."

When we got there, we discovered a somewhat down-at-heel troupe, but none the less enthusiastic and committed for that. The performers included a small team of musicians and their conductor, a handful of clowns of various degrees of grotesqueness, a pair of aerial performers, a stage magician with assistant, two animal handlers, and the obligatory grandiose Ringmaster.

The performance was well-attended, and the audience seemed pleased enough as it unfolded along its predictable lines. During the trapeze act, something seemed to startle Holmes, and he snapped out of his inattentive reverie, leaning forward suddenly. Less than a minute later, tragedy struck. One of the trapeze artists mistimed his leap, and plummeted to the floor. The audience dissolved into a shrieking mass as the Beethoven screeched to a halt, and loud wails of anguish burst from the magician's assistant. I pushed my way into the ring, but it was hopeless.

"I'm afraid he's dead," I said to the horrified Ringmaster.

"Murdered," added Holmes, just behind me.

The Ringmaster and I spun round to look at him.

"Yes, murdered," Holmes said. "And we all watched the villain kill him, and did nothing."

What did he mean?

SOLUTION ON PAGE

THE FIRST PORTMANTEAU

I was taking my ease one evening in Baker Street, following a rather delightful dinner of stuffed quail that Mrs. Hudson had prepared for Sherlock Holmes and myself. I had thought that Holmes was conducting some abstruse chemical experiment or other, but was disabused of that notion when he appeared beside me and wordlessly handed me a rather eccentric illustration, which I have diligently copied below.

I recognised it for what it was, of course. "This is one of your devilish picture puzzles," said I.

"I see nothing escapes you," Holmes replied with a twinkle.

"So I am to consider each separate element of the image as a clue, and deduce the only possible location that fits all the evidence."

"You are," Holmes agreed. "If you are so able. Restrict your considerations to London however, Watson."

I gave it some thought, and was finally able to pronounce a solution which Holmes would accept. Where does the picture refer to?

SOLUTION ON PAGE 110

39

URCHINS

Wiggins was with us, receiving a briefing for a sensitive mission of observation. Holmes was most insistent that he go to extraordinary steps to avoid detection.

"I want you to use nine lads, Wiggins. Send them out in groups of three. You'll need to have them venture forth for six days. To help avoid detection though, I do not want any two boys next to each other twice. You may place them in the same group a second time, so long as they are not adjacent to someone they have been adjacent to before."

"No problem, Mr. Holmes," said the urchin, "just as you like." He sounded confident.

Could you have matched Holmes' instructions?

SOLUTION ON PAGE 110

THE MEADOW OF DEATH

"A couple were found dead in a quiet valley in the Highlands," Holmes said to me one morning, apropos of nothing.

"They were murdered, I assume?" It was rather rare for Holmes to take interest in cases where foul play was not involved.

"It seems not," was his surprising reply. "They were found lying next to each other, hand in hand, in a pleasant field carpeted with new spring flowers. There was no sign of whatever it was that killed them. They were less than a mile to the nearest village. There was no evidence of any sort of murderous assault, no broken limbs, nor any of the tell-tale signs that suicide might have left. Lightning would have left char marks, rocks would have caused clearly visible wounds, and the physicians found no evidence of poisons or disease. They did not appear to have been robbed, either. I have an idea, of course. But what do you make of it?"

SOLUTION ON PAGE 111

The Third Literal Oddity

Finding myself at an idle moment on a quiet September afternoon, I asked Holmes if he happened to have any little word trial prepared which he had been saving up to vex me with. That may strike you as a little masochistic, but I was looking for a diversion.

He searched his memory for a moment, and nodded. "I'll offer you 'regimentations' and the mineral 'nitromagnesite'. What distinguishes them?"

SOLUTION ON PAGE 111

GOLD

Holmes and I apprehended a vicious gold-smuggler in Epping one nasty September evening. He was a particularly unpleasant sort, and it was a genuine pleasure to hand him over to Scotland Yard.

He had been in the middle of preparing a consignment of gold slabs for shipment to France – 800 of them, each one 11" wide, 12½" long, and 1" deep. A king's ransom indeed.

Holmes pointed out to my attention that the box he had packed them in was square, and sufficiently high that it exactly contained all of the slabs with no wasted space left over. Furthermore, less than a dozen of the slabs had been stood on an edge.

Can you discern the dimensions of the box?

SOLUTION ON PAGE 112

STONES

One pleasant Sunday afternoon, Holmes had the Irregulars gather him up a basket of precisely fifty stones. Then starting from the step of 221b Baker Street, towards St. John's Wood, Holmes started laying the stones out with an ever increasing gap between them. He placed the second stone one yard from the first, the third three yards from the second, the fourth five yards from the third, and the fifth seven yards from the fourth.

At this point, he returned to where the rest of us were standing, watching him curiously.

"Young Wiggins, what would you say if I told you that I would place all fifty stones according to this pattern, and then pay you a farthing to pick them back up – but strictly one at a time, bringing each back to the basket here at the start before going to fetch the next?"

"I'd tell you to bugger off, Mr. Holmes, Sir."

Holmes laughed. "Quite right too."

But why?

SOLUTION ON PAGE 112

HUDSONS TANGLED

"I've mentioned my niece Katie to you, I believe," said Mrs. Hudson to Sherlock Holmes one morning.

"Indeed," said Holmes. "She works for the family with the eccentric twins."

"That's her. She has a younger sister, Alison. Their ages can be a bit of a tangle."

"How so?" I asked.

Mrs. Hudson smiled, and took a deep breath. "Counted together, they are forty-four years of age. Katie is twice as old as Alison was when Katie was half as old as Alison will be when Alison is three times as old as Katie was when Katie was three times as old as Alison."

Can you tell how old Katie is?

SOLUTION ON PAGE 113

The Second Curiosity

Shortly after Christmas one year, I was relaxing and enjoying the season when Holmes' thoughts turned to the tragic Massacre of the Innocents, King Herod's vile infanticide which we remember on December 28th.

"It is said," Holmes mused, "that after the deed, a number of the unfortunate mites were buried in sand, with only their feet sticking up to indicate their presence. How do you imagine that they told the boys apart from the girls, on such scant evidence?"

SOLUTION ON PAGE 114

Fencing

"A good detective must be a man of science, Watson."

I of course agree with this sentiment, and said so. Among the many things that my time with Sherlock Holmes has taught me is the paramount importance of even the most seemingly irrelevant physical clue.

"What do you know of the science of acoustics?"

"As much as any common lay-man," I allowed. "I'm confident in saying that the old folk myth about a duck's quack having no echo is utter bunk, and physically impossible besides."

"Imagine you are putting up wooden fence posts in a large field, perhaps to prepare an enclosure for sheep."

"Very well." I duly complied, painting the scene with a little light drizzle, and a hilly backdrop.

"When you start, near a stone building, you can hear a clear echo coming back to you. Later, near the middle of the field, the hammering noise you make is dull and flat. But later still, in another part of the field, you can hear a clear ringing noise. Do you know what could cause such an effect?"

SOLUTION ON PAGE 114

THE SOHO PIT

We were walking through the Soho area of London one morning, in search of one of Holmes' less reputable contacts. As we strolled down Dean Street, we passed a workman engaged in digging a hole for some purpose or other.

"You, sir, are five feet and ten inches in height," Holmes declared to him.

The man nodded. "And when I've gone twice as deep as I am now, then my head will be twice as far below the level of the pavement as it is above it this instant."

Holmes told the fellow how deep his hole was going to be, and got a respectful nod in return. Could you have done so?

SOLUTION ON PAGE 115

The Second Mental Trial

"I have decided that today I know two hypothetical men, my dear Watson. Alfie and Bill."

"As you wish, Holmes," I said. "What do they look like?"

"Fishmongers," said he.

"So. Alright, I'm picturing a pair of hypothetical fish-mongers."

"It matters little, in truth. The case is that Alfie has twice as many sisters as he has brothers, whilst his sister Mary has the same number of sisters and brothers. Bill, by comparison, has three times as many sisters as brothers, but his sister Nancy has the same ratio of brothers to sisters as Mary does. Assuming both have just the bare amount of siblings required to fulfil their conditions, who has the more brothers, Alfie or Bill?"

SOLUTION ON PAGE

The Hanged Man

A rather perplexing crime had prompted Scotland Yard to summon Mr. Sherlock Holmes and myself to Draper Street. A temperamental young artist of some promise had been found hanged, and the police were at a loss to explain the murder.

His absence around town having been noted, the young man had been discovered in his rooms, behind doors so firmly locked and bolted that it took three stout constables to batter them open. The window was similarly secure, and anyway, it looked straight down onto the road some four stories below. The body itself was hanging by a short cord from a light fitting in the ceiling, nothing but air and dark carpet beneath its booted feet. In fact, there was no object whatsoever in evidence that the young man could possibly have stood upon with which to take his own life. The room was perfectly tidy, and the maid assured us that everything looked to be in its usual order, with nothing missing, and no additions. The police were certain that the killer had tidied up after the murder, but didn't know how he had exited the room.

Sherlock Holmes walked through the door, glanced around once, and snorted in derision. He knelt by the corpse, touched the carpet, and then rose again. "Really, Lestrade," he said, drying his fingers on his handkerchief. "You've excelled yourself this time. The situation is perfectly clear."

Would you consider it so?

SOLUTION ON PAGE 116

HAPPY FAMILY

A brief visit from Mrs. Hudson, with a nice pot of tea, prompted Sherlock Holmes to unleash an unusually fiendish little puzzle upon me.

"Our redoubtable Mrs. Hudson believes her family to be a complicated tangle, but honestly she could be much worse off."

"Oh, really?" I asked, innocently.

"Very much so," Holmes said. "Imagine a family friend being presented with the children of a house as follows. First a boy and a girl are brought in, let us call them Amelia and Barney. The friend is informed that Barney is twice Amelia's age. Then a second girl, Charlotte, arrives, and brings the total of the girls' ages to twice that of Barney's. After her comes another boy, Daniel, and his presence brings the combined ages of the boys to twice that of the girls. The final clincher is the arrival of the last child, Emily, on the occasion of her 21st birthday. Her presence swings the age total back, so that the combined ages of the girls is again twice that of the boys."

"It sounds a beastly business."

"Particularly, my dear Watson, when I ask you to tell me how old each of the children are."

SOLUTION ON PAGE 116

The Barn

Norfolk was the setting for this particular problem. Inspector Lestrade brought word to Baker Street one chilly February morning that a colleague of his up in King's Lynn was having persistent trouble with a raider who specialised in robbing the warehouses of the shipping companies out there. The investigation had been proceeding well, until a sinister incident unnerved the superstitious local constabulary enough that help had to be sought. Perhaps inevitably, the problem found its way to Mr. Sherlock Holmes.

The villain had struck on a snowy Friday night, and made off unseen with a substantial quantity of goods. Witness statements suggested the villain had headed west out of the town, and once the storm had abated, and dawn had broken, the police found a crisp, deep hoof-print trail clearly leading over the fields. They followed the prints to a disused barn, steeled themselves, and threw open the door, ready to apprehend the thief.

The barn, however, was empty, save for a few small discarded bits of farming equipment. The snow was deep enough that even a sparrow's passing would be clearly noted. There were no drag-marks where prints could have been eliminated. There were no other ways out of the barn. The raider had ridden into the barn and vanished into thin air, according to the disturbed constables, "like the very Devil himself."

Holmes listened to Lestrade's tale, and just arched an eyebrow, clearly amused. The inspector's wounded expression simply made Holmes's eyes twinkle all the more. Can you explain?

SOLUTION ON PAGE 117

FIENDISH PUZZLES

"My mind rebels at stagnation.
Give me problems, give me work...
I abhor the dull routine of existence.
I crave for mental exaltation."

Sherlock Holmes

The Third Mental Trial

"My hypothetical friends, Alfie and Bill, have an acquaintance," Holmes said to me one afternoon. I understood this to mean that he had another mental challenge for me.

"Soon you will have an entirely hypothetical village," I said.

"That may happen, my dear Watson. But today, we are concerned just with the addition of Charlie. Poor Charlie has run out of lamp oil at an inopportune moment. Alfie and Bill both have reasonable stocks – Alfie has eight pints, and Bill has five. The two decide that the comradely thing to do would be to pool their oil, and divide it up into thirds. This they do, and to repay their kindness, Charlie hands over thirteen farthings."

"Who will be their next friend?" I asked. "David?"

"Unlikely," said Holmes. "But for now, in the interests of equity, tell me, how should the money be divided?

SOLUTION ON PAGE 120

IN PARIS

"You may recall that the World's Fair was held in Paris a few years back," Holmes said.

I nodded. "Quite the show."

"Quite. Did you hear about the missing brother?"

"No?" I leaned forward, curiosity engaged.

"A funny business. An American lady and her brother arrived at the Ritz the afternoon before the fair, and checked in to their rooms. They had dinner together, but the lady was tired, and her brother flat-out exhausted, so they called it an early night.

"The next morning, the lady was surprised that her brother did not appear at their agreed-upon time for breakfast. She asked the waiter if he had already eaten, and received just a puzzled stare. When she went looking for his room, number 13, she was unable to find it, and had to seek help from the staff. The concierge superciliously informed her that there was no Room 13. The manager, when he appeared, said the same. All the staff insisted she had arrived alone and eaten alone the night before. The registry book showed just her name. The rooms on the first floor went straight from 12 to 14. Despite her very great distress, she could find no evidence her brother had ever existed."

"My word," I said, perplexed.

"What do you suppose was going on?"

SOLUTION ON PAGE 120

POP POP

"Have you seen one of these before, Watson?"

Holmes handed me a small tin boat. It looked unremarkable at first glance, but on closer inspection, I discovered what appeared to be a small boiler set-up in the wheelhouse, and a pipe protruding out of the back. I admitted that the thing was unfamiliar.

"A clever Frenchman has designed it," Holmes said. "A child's toy. You prime the mechanism with a little water, light the small spirit burner, and then place it in a bathtub or paddling pool or what have you. Once the boiler has warmed up, the toy will propel itself across the surface. It accelerates in little fits and starts, emitting a popping noise as it does so."

"Ingenious," I said.

"Yes, quite. How do you imagine that it works? That pipe is the sole egress from the boiler."

SOLUTION ON PAGE 121

EVASION

"See if you can do something with this little bit of chronological evasion," Holmes said to me one afternoon.

"I'll try," I promised.

"A man and a woman are discussing their respective ages. Their combined age is 49, and they come to the conclusion that when the man was the age that the woman is now, he was at that time twice as old as she was."

"I see."

"Do you? How old are the pair now?"

SOLUTION ON PAGE 122

Six-Sided Dice

"A simple little question for you, Watson."

Holmes tossed me a standard die, which I caught.

"The humble die conceals many mysteries and is at the heart of many adventures. Given that each pair of opposite faces on the die must always add up to seven, how many different ways are there to set out the numbers on three separate dice?

SOLUTION ON PAGE 122

The Fourth Mental Trial

"Are you ready to give your mind a stern lexical test, Watson?"

I confessed that 'stern' sounded a little daunting, but so long as there was no dire penalty for failure, I was prepared to do my best.

"That's the spirit, old chap. The nine-letter word 'checkbook', an American coinage from our own 'chequebook', possesses an unusual quality. This is shared with a small number of other words, all shorter, including our very own 'exceeded'. What do you imagine that it is?"

SOLUTION ON PAGE 123

THE DICTIONARY

I watched curiously as Holmes fished a number of books out from the shelves in his study. The books were of a size, which I quickly determined had been the primary motivation for their selection. Holmes brought them over, and popped them down on the table at my elbow.

"You have here a stack of books, numbering half a dozen in total," he declared.

"Indeed so," said I.

"It is of course possible to edge the stack out slightly, so that the second book protrudes a little further than the first. I've placed the books up against the very edge of the table. Do you imagine that it is possible to arrange the stack I have provided you with in such a way that one – or more – of the books is hanging completely over the table?"

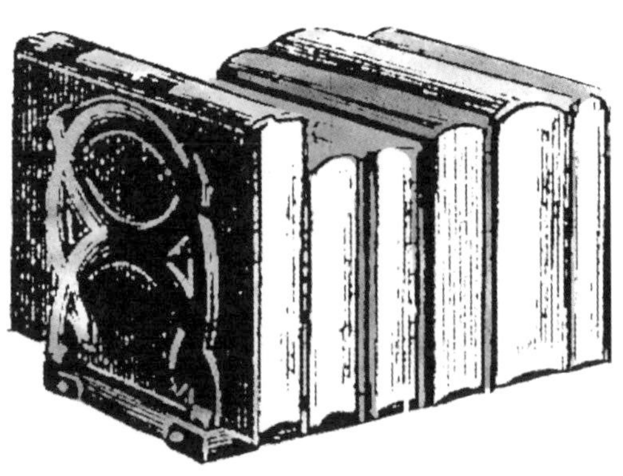

SOLUTION ON PAGE

THE THIRD CURIOSITY

"Girdle the Earth!" "What?" I snapped to attention, reasonably startled.

"In your mind, man. Girdle the Earth. With steel, I dare say, for structure. Now assuming – fallaciously, of course – that the Earth were perfectly flat and round around the equator so such a girdle could be circular, place it so that it is exactly flush with the Earth."

I complied.

"Now, if you added six yards to the length of that girdle, how far do you suppose that would raise it off the surface?"

SOLUTION ON PAGE 124

The Fish Murder

A regular police patrol found Mister Frank Hale gasping his very last breath in the streets surrounding Billingsgate Fish Market in the early hours. He had been stabbed through the neck, and clearly it had happened very recently. On the basis that his killer had to still be nearby, the constables chased down and apprehended the only other fellow on the street.

Like Hale, Rick Weir was a fish merchant, and the police were able to show that the pair were at least rivals professionally. Under questioning, Weir maintained total ignorance of the event, and claimed that he had fled the police simply out of an instinct born from confusion. As evidence of his innocence, he pointed out that he had nothing on his person that could remotely be used as a murder weapon, nor had he discarded any such item. The police searched the area thoroughly, but could find nothing that might have plausibly caused Hale's rather irregularly-shaped wound.

With nothing more to go on than the victim's damp shirt collar and ragged stab-wound, Scotland Yard was on the verge of allowing Weir his freedom. It was at that point that Holmes heard of the case, and scribbled a quick note to Inspector Lestrade. Weir was formally charged with the murder in less than an hour.

Can you imagine what thought had occurred to my companion?

SOLUTION ON PAGE 124

A Hearty Drop

"My hypothetical friend Alfie," Holmes said, "wishes to divide a keg of ale equitably between Bill, Charlie and himself."

"I dare say he does," I retorted. "That undoubtedly explains his hat problem."

Holmes was unruffled. "The keg contains a whole six quarts, but the men find themselves with just a 2½ quart pail and a three-pint pickling jar, fortunately both perfectly clean."

"Can you not imagine them a hypothetical pint glass?"

"I cannot," Holmes replied. "That being so, can you tell me how they might most efficiently divide and consume the ale so that each gets his four pints?"

SOLUTION ON PAGE

THE BOX

Holmes took delivery of a jar of chemicals, and once he had it stowed away safely, tossed the box to me.

I caught it automatically. It seemed a rather plain affair.

"That box has a top that is 120 inches square. The side is 96 inches square, and the end is 80 inches square. What are its dimensions?"

SOLUTION ON PAGE 126

SHEEP

"Sometimes, my dear Watson, you have to think outside the boundaries of the sheep pen."

"A curious turn of phrase, old friend."

"But deliberate," Holmes said. "You have four sheep pens of equal size. How would you place fifteen sheep to ensure that each pen contained the same number of sheep?"

I thought about it for a little while. "It seems impossible, without butchering a sheep."

"Such exertions are unnecessary," said Holmes, "but do not forget my earlier admonition."

SOLUTION ON PAGE 126

The Second Portmanteau

"I have another picture for you to puzzle over, Watson."

Sherlock Holmes passed me the extraordinary illustration which I have reproduced here.

"It contains all the visual clues you could possibly require to positively identify one particular spot in London. When you can place the relevance of each element of the picture, you will be able to allow no possible doubt regarding the location to which it refers. Be stout; the solution is not quite as obvious as some of the other images I have passed you."

I turned my attention from my friend to the drawing he had given me. To where does it refer?

SOLUTION ON PAGE 127

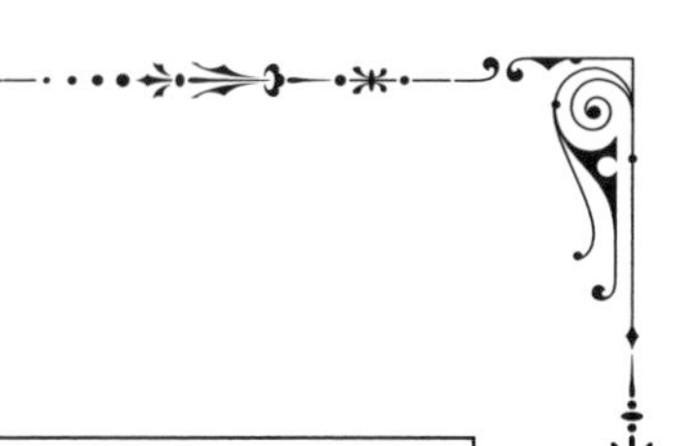

GET A HAT

"My hypothetical friend Alfie's dinner party had six guests," Holmes said. "That meant that there were seven hats. By the time it came to depart, the men were too wearied by their exertions at the table to take notice of which hat they obtained."

"No doubt," I replied. "I suspect any normal man would be fatigued by an evening in your prodigious mind, my dear Holmes."

"Perhaps," he replied. "But either way, the truth is that after all had left, no man had the correct hat, not even Alfie. How many possible variations are there of this mishap?"

SOLUTION ON PAGE 128

Nephews

We were in the area near King's Cross railway station one morning, pursuing a matter involving a larcenous baker's nephew. I should make it clear that the larceny was on the baker's part; the nephew was quite innocent. As that may be, I was deep in thought when Holmes said to me, "Watson old chap, do you know that it is possible to be both the nephew and uncle of a fellow at the same time?"

That brought me up short. "Surely not," I protested.

"Oh yes," Holmes said. "All perfectly within the law, too."

"How can that be?"

"Why don't you tell me," he replied.

SOLUTION ON PAGE 128

The Fifth Mental Trial

"I have another mental exercise for you, my friend."

I looked up from my book. "Very well, my dear Holmes. I'm sure it is to my benefit."

"Immeasurably," came the reply. "Consider for a moment that you have been given a counterfeit shilling in amongst your money. It is ever so slightly lighter than it ought to be, but it is otherwise indistinguishable from the real thing. You cannot tell by hand, but you have a balance scale. What is the least number of weighings that you can perform upon the scale to discover the precise identity of the counterfeit?"

SOLUTION ON PAGE 129

Equity

"I have an amusing little test of your mathematical faculties here, my dear Watson."

I suppressed a sigh, and girded my mental loins. "Indeed?"

"You may have noticed that the even digits, 2, 4, 6 and 8, add up to 20, whilst the odd digits, 1, 3, 5, 7 and 9, add up to 25. It's the unpaired 5 that makes the difference."

"I'm with you so far," I said.

"Excellent. Can you contrive a way to arrange these two sets of digits into additive sums which total an identical amount? You are allowed to use simple vulgar fractions if you wish, but nothing more complex than that, and the only mathematical operand available to you is addition."

"May I have some paper and a pencil?" I asked.

"Naturally," Holmes said.

What was the solution?

SOLUTION ON PAGE 129

Twenty Thousand Leagues

"As I recall Watson, you've read Mr. Verne's tale about Captain Nemo and his miraculous underwater submersible, the Nautilus."

I nodded. "I have. I enjoyed it, but I fear that it would offer you little. The villainies it contains have little mystery to them."

"So I gather," said Holmes. "Although I believe the French are currently testing a similar – if much less fanciful – device with a marked degree of success. I cannot help feeling that the captain of any such device would spend his entire time living in mortal terror of accidentally touching the bottom of the ocean."

"The risk of damage to the structure, you mean?"

"Well yes, there is that, but no, I was thinking of a danger that would apply to the mildest sandy bottom as much as to a jagged shelf. More so, even."

What did he mean?

SOLUTION ON PAGE 130

The Shoreditch Bank

Sherlock Holmes and myself encountered a cunning method of bank robbery in Shoreditch on one memorable occasion. The manager was diligent in his security arrangements. The bank's safe was a massive thing, complex enough that even a skilled thief would take an hour or more to get into it, and this with cutting tools that would leave very obvious scarring. This in turn was locked in the manager's office. The office door had a small viewing port set into in. The guards' rounds of the bank brought them past the manager's office every six minutes, and they always paused for a moment to peer through the port and inspect the safe.

Despite these precautions, when the cleaning lady went into the manager's office early on Monday morning, to start tidying up before the week began, she immediately realised that the bank had been burgled. The security men were utterly confounded, they and their colleagues having faithfully checked the safe every few minutes, all through the weekend. Given the length of time that it would have taken for the safe to be opened, and the regularity of the guards' observations, can you imagine how the criminals had found the time to get it open?

SOLUTION ON PAGE 130

MARKHAM

"A very simple matter this one, Watson." Holmes indicated an illustration on his desk, which outlined the details from the scene of the recent Markham murder. "I feel confident that even you should be able to see through to the heart of the crime."

I reminded him that I was not familiar with the particulars of the case.

"Markham was in his study, working. His wife was in the drawing room, and has said that although her husband had been a little preoccupied recently, she had no idea that he was in danger. She realised that she could hear conversation through the wall: her husband sounding agitated, and a rougher man's voice which she could not clearly make out. Then there was a blood-curdling scream, a heavy thump, and silence. She rushed to the study door in a panic, but finding it locked on the inside, dashed out and around the side of the house to the study window. It too was locked tight, and the curtains drawn. Her statement is corroborated by the maid.

"Her cries for help brought the assistance of the police, who battered down the door and found the room as shown, and the window still firmly locked and barred from the inside. Markham was dead of course, with a hunting knife through his heart. Both the widow and the maid insist that no intruder could have escaped without their notice, and the police admit that they can find no signs of egress.

"So tell me. Who killed Markham?"

MONTENEGRO

Holmes made the acquaintance of a pair of charming rogues from Montenegro at one point, and, I gather, obtained all sorts of useful tid-bits from them. One of the items that he obtained was a curious little dice game.

The game is played with three regular six-sided dice. Each player selects two separate odd numbers that the three dice sum to. The four numbers must all be different, so in fairness, they take turns to select their numbers. They then throw the dice alternately; whoever throws one of their numbers first wins, although the opponent has one last chance to throw their own number and make for a draw.

The question is whether it is possible for the two players to have exactly identical odds of winning the game.

SOLUTION ON PAGE 132

WORDPLAY

"You may take the letters from A through to O," Holmes informed me suddenly.

"That's very kind of you," I replied. "But whatever do you mean?"

"I wish you to combine those letters into groups of three, so that no two letters ever share the same group twice. It is possible to form a clear 35 groups without any of them ever having a repeated letter pairing."

"Very well," I replied.

"That is not the challenge, however. The challenge is to form as many common 3-letter English words as possible within those 35 groups. Abbreviations and proper nouns are to be discounted, I'm afraid."

How well can you do?

SOLUTION ON PAGE 132

WIMBLEDON COMMON

Holmes turned to me with a wry smile and tapped his Morning Post. "In here, Watson, we have the story of a cabbie who picked up a fare in Putney yesterday morning, took the fellow out into Wimbledon Common, and then bludgeoned him to death with a cudgel he kept under his seat. Why do you suppose he did so?"

"A vicious mugging?"

"Not so; the corpse was found with wallet and all effects."

"Some bad blood, then?"

"The two men had never even heard of each other before, let alone laid eyes on each other."

I thought for a moment. "Well, is the driver just demented?"

"Not a bit of it," said Holmes. "He is entirely rational, and has an explanation that he clearly feels justified his action. He will undoubtedly swing for it, although they might be more lenient if he were tried in Paris."

Can you guess what the reason was?

SOLUTION ON PAGE 133

The Sixth Mental Trial

"Let us return one more time to my hypothetical friends, Alfie and Bill. Imagine that you are with the pair of them in the office of a curious prison warder. Charlie's presence is not required."

"I am in prison with a pair of fishmongers," I noted.

"You are all innocent, of course," Holmes replied. "Sad victims of a miscarriage of justice, fear not."

"My mind is at ease."

"Capital. The warder shows you all five coloured signs, two black and three white. He then has you turn around in a line, and affixes a sign to the back of each of your prison uniforms. The warder informs you that the first man to correctly identify the colour of his sign will walk free; but identify wrongly, or collude, and your sentence will be extended. Then he allows you to turn around and inspect each other. You see that both Alfie and Bill are wearing white signs. The other two look at you, and at each other. What colour is your sign?"

SOLUTION ON PAGE 134

MOST IRREGULAR

It was Wiggins' precocity that first won him his exalted position at the head of the Baker Street Irregulars. When Holmes first encountered the urchin, he enquired as to the lad's age.

Rather than give a straight answer, the deviousness of Wiggins' reply earned Holmes' interest. "It's like this," he said. "The year I was born, David, the deacon now at Paddington Green, was just one quarter of the age of Father Anthony, and now he is a third of the age of Father Gary. I'm only a quarter as old as Father Anthony is now, but in four more years I'll be a quarter as old as Father Gary will be."

How old was Wiggins?

SOLUTION ON PAGE 135

Carl Black

"**D**id you see the item about the death of Carl Black, Watson?"

"Who?"

"A former steel baron from New York. He was kidnapped last year by Serbian radicals during an exploratory business trip to the area, and ransomed for a very princely sum. He was lucky. Many such victims are never returned. Black resigned from the company immediately afterwards, although of course the firm's travel insurance covered the actual cost, and he moved to the south of France."

"Was he murdered?"

"No. Boating accident. A bit of foolishness, with serious consequences, but nothing in the least bit sinister about it."

"Oh," I said, increasingly mystified.

"Note that Black's former company was in good financial shape for the first time in five years, and that although relations were cordial, he had possessed no formal ties to them for almost twelve months. The interesting question then becomes, why was his former business partner caught trying to burn down Black's chateau three nights later?"

A good question.

SOLUTION ON PAGE 136

A Matter of Time

"Come, Watson," said Holmes to me one afternoon. "Indulge me in a little matter of creative thought."

"Of course," I replied, with just a hint of trepidation.

"Suppose you need to exactly measure the passage of 45 minutes before making a timely entrance. You are required to wait in some dreary room, without a pocket-watch or convenient clock. You do, however, have two lengths of tallow-dipped stick, and a box of matches. The sticks are certain to burn for an hour precisely, but they will not do so at a constant rate.

"Variations in thickness and other defects of construction mean that after 30 minutes, just a small length of stick may be consumed, or alternately a great length. There is no guarantee that the pattern will be the same from one stick to the other. Yet these inadequate sticks are all you have at your disposal. How then would you use them to measure the time correctly?"

How indeed?

SOLUTION ON PAGE 136

THE FAULTY WATCH

"Let us suppose your watch is faulty, my dear Watson."

"You know very well that it is not," I replied.

"I do indeed, but for the sake of discussion, let us pretend that it is so."

"Very well."

"You have made some notes, and you are aware that the minute and hour hand on your watch meet precisely once every sixty-four minutes. Is your watch gaining time, or losing it?"

SOLUTION ON PAGE

137

A Puzzling Portmanteau

"Another of your damnable images, Holmes?" My eager expression removed any sting the words might have seemed to carry. The truth was, I rather enjoyed poring over the things.

"Yes indeed, old friend. This one should provide you with a genuine challenge, too. Each aspect of the picture is a carefully-crafted clue. Taken together, all the clues point to just one place in London. This is the last of them for now, so I have naturally saved the best for the occasion."

He handed me the drawing, which I have replicated for you to examine. "Thank you, Holmes."

"You are of course welcome, but I'd not be too hasty. You may be cursing me before you solve this one."

It took a while, but I did indeed crack the mystery. Can you?

SOLUTION ON PAGE 137

THE LADIES OF MORDEN

The Ladies of the Morden whist circle came to our attention in regard to a daring little robbery that had occurred in Balham. The case was solved easily, but Holmes was more interested in their playing regimen.

There were twelve ladies, and they so arranged themselves that over eleven evenings, each of them played no more than once with the same lady as a partner, nor more than twice with the same lady as an opponent. By this, they managed to ensure that every member played every other member in all possible quadrants.

Can you work out how such a thing might be achieved?

SOLUTION ON PAGE 138

A Fascinating Curiosity

"Tell me, Watson. Do you imagine that a perfect billiard table is absolutely level?"

"Of course," I replied.

"Oh? How curious. Would you like to guess why you are wrong?"

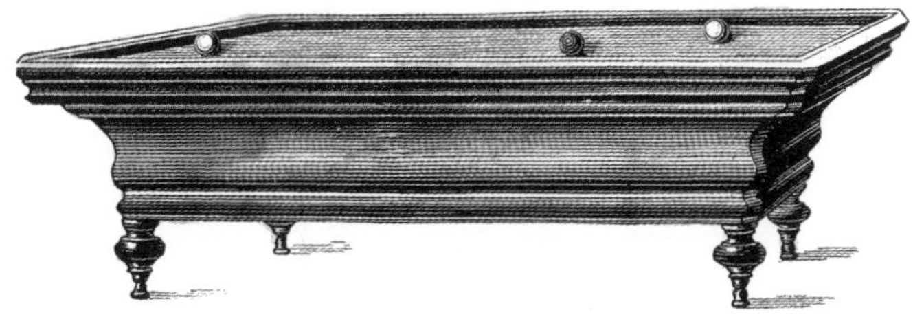

SOLUTION ON PAGE 139

GROUPS

One evening I found myself between relaxations, and Holmes seized the opportunity to spring a rather devilish little mathematical oddity upon me. All in the name of improving my mental acuity, you understand.

"Take the nine digits," he instructed me. "Set them out once and once alone in three groups – a single digit, and two groups of four digits. Taking each group as a number, the groups must obey the stricture that the first group multiplied by the second group will equal the third group. Some methodical enquiry will be required."

Can you find the answer?

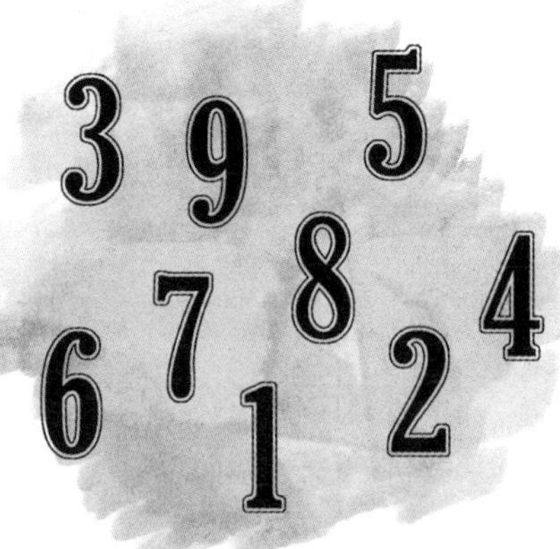

SOLUTION ON PAGE 139

The Eggtimer's Companion

In the course of the rather odd affair of the Eggtimer's Companion, Holmes and I came across a pair of feuding families in Highgate, the Adamses and the Southwells. Both families consisted of a mother, father and two children, and it was interesting to note that the sum totals of the ages of each family was 100 years.

The coincidence was increased by the fact that in both families, the daughter of the house was older than her brother, and if you added the squares of the ages of the mother, daughter and son together, you would get a total which exactly matched the square of the age of the father.

Miss Southwell was one year older than her brother however, whilst Miss Adams was two years older than hers. Armed with that knowledge, Holmes maintained, it was perfectly possible to discern the age of each of the eight individuals.

Can you deduce the ages?

SOLUTION ON PAGE  140

A Curious Mental Trial

"I'd like you to consider the following sequence of numbers, Watson. They are: 2, 5, 8, 11, 16, 14. What number less than 20 is the next in the line? I assure you that you do not need any mathematical aptitude to arrive at the correct answer."

2, 5, 8, 11, 16, 14...

SOLUTION ON PAGE 140

Cones

Holmes approached me one lunchtime bearing a simple conical funnel and a determined expression. "I have a littletrial for you, my dear Watson."

"By all means," I replied.

He passed me the cone. "If this funnel were a solid cone, it would be possible to whittle a straight cylinder out of it by removing the top, and then cutting straight down from the circular intersection."

"Very true," I observed.

"If I cut near the bottom, I would get a short, thick cylinder. If I cut near the top, it would be tall and thin."

"Yes, I can see that."

"So where would I cut to get the cylinder of the greatest volume?"

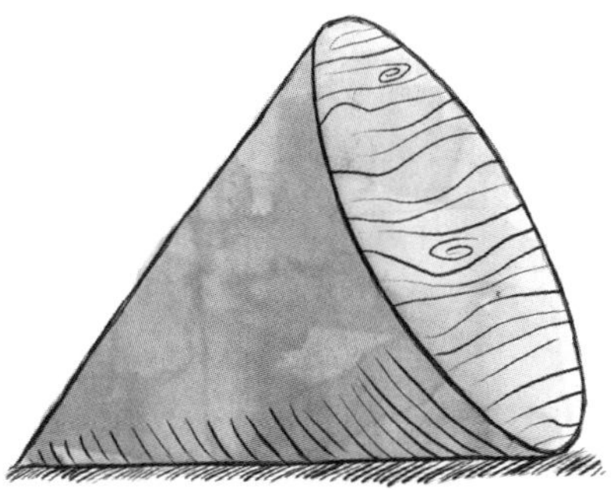

SOLUTION ON PAGE 141

Down on the Farm

I remember one particular occasion that pulled Holmes and myself out to an uninspiring pasture in West Sussex. A local farmer had noticed his sheep behaving oddly, and on investigation discovered a body in the middle of his field, in seemingly undisturbed grass. The body had been moved, but of course we had to slog out through the summer sun to examine the site. While we were looking around, Holmes discovered the top half of an unlit match, which he declared to have come from the corpse by dint of position and freshness.

A short while later, we got to examine the body itself, which had been moved to a more suitable location. He had been a middle-aged fellow, clearly of some means. Cause of death appeared to be general physical trauma, which included crushed ribs, smashed jaw and broken legs as well as the skull damage which had most probably finished him. He was dressed in soft shoes, stout woollen trousers and a sturdy leather jacket trimmed with fur. He had no personal possessions however, not even a watch.

Holmes took one look at his bootlaces and declared the man to be a Prussian, and then remarked that the style of his hair indicated he had been passing himself off as British, so he was probably a spy.

So declaring, he then asserted that the reason – and method – of his death were painfully obvious. Can you work out what he meant?

SOLUTION ON PAGE

BOARD

"I say, Watson." I looked up from my book. "Yes, Holmes?"

"I have a little challenge for you, simple in the telling, but less so in the execution. There are 64 squares on a chessboard, but how many different squares and rectangles can one or more of those squares be formed into?"

SOLUTION ON PAGE 142

The Night Watchman

We were called to the scene of a violent robbery down by the Thames, where a hapless night watchman had been murdered, and a consignment of shipped goods stolen. The poor watchman was dumped in the river after being killed, and the water immediately caused his pocket watch to stop working.

That would have given the time of the robbery, had one foolish policeman not tried to get the watch working again, and scrambled the time. Holmes was furious of course, but all the unfortunately constable could recall was that the second-hand had just passed 49, and that the hour and minute hand were perfectly aligned together.

Holmes recognized that the hands on the watch were of the constantly sweeping variety, rather than the type which clicks from division to division, and declared that this made the time of the robbery perfectly obvious.

What was the time on the watch when it stopped?

SOLUTION ON PAGE

A Literal Oddity

"I have saved the best for the end," Holmes declared.

I felt my eyebrows raise. "What's that?"

"One final trial of your authorial muscle, Watson."

"Ah. If it is anything like the last..."

Holmes shook his head. "Not a bit of it. This one will genuinely tax your ingenuity."

"Very well," I replied, with a little trepidation.

"I want you to find me an English word which has each of its letters repeated exactly three times. I'll warn you now that I know of only one, and its etymology suggests an Italian derivation. I would discount any contrived word which was simply the same syllable repeated three times as being an unworthy answer."

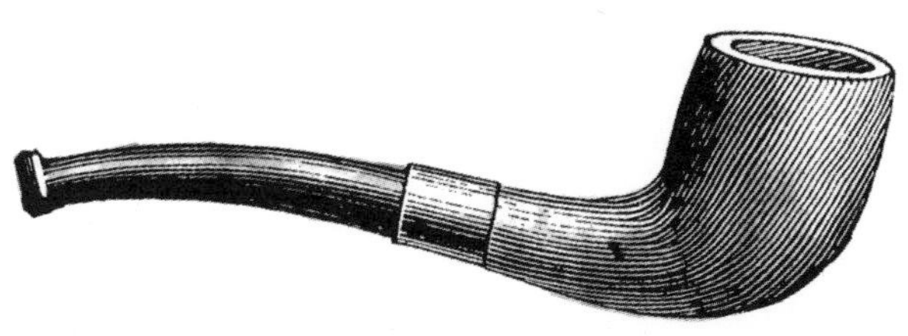

SOLUTION ON PAGE 143

CUNNING

ANSWERS & SOLUTIONS

"I cannot live without brain-work. What else is there to live for?"

Sherlock Holmes

The Statuette

"Watson old chap, you'd best stick to medicine," Holmes said. "The two men were in cahoots. The pair pick a likely item. One buys it and talks up the value of its twin, and then the other sells it back again to the same dealer, at great profit. They split the proceeds, and when the poor dealer comes hoping to sell what he thinks is the companion piece, his original client has moved on. Instead of making £800, he has lost £200. The pair were only caught in their deception because they became greedy, and tried two such stings in London in too short a space of time.

Cold Hands

"There are two factors responsible for the cool effect of the vigorous breath. One is evaporation. As the air blows across your skin, higher-energy water molecules evaporate off. This reduces the average energy of the remaining molecules, and brings down their temperature, cooling you. This process occurs more rapidly with a harder breath, chiefly because the increased speed of the air encourages more of your sweat to make the leap to the gaseous state.

"The other, more minor, factor is gaseous expansion. As the breath comes from between your pursed lips, it spreads out from that tight position you had it in. The act of occupying a greater space reduces its temperature, for certain, somewhat abstract reasons. This means that the air actually is a little cooler."

DEDICATION

I am, of course, talking about clocks - ranging in number of components from hourglasses, with their myriad of sand grains, down to the good old sundial. Grandfather clocks can be far larger than a man, whilst some truly miniscule hourglasses are available.

GRAINS OF SAND

The simple answer is that no, for the bulk of the time, the weight of the glass will not be affected. The missing weight from the falling sand is counterbalanced by the extra downward pressure from the grains which strike the bottom. There is a slight lessening of weight as the sand first starts to fall, before any has hit the floor, and a concomitant slight gain of weight at the end, when there is no sand remaining to start falling, but not all of it has landed yet.

The Green Stone

Although my friend's powers of deduction are utterly beyond me, I was able to discern what he was getting at on this occasion. The poison was in the ice of the first drink they were served. Rebecca drank hers quickly, before the ice had been given sufficient time to melt, and escaped harm. His husband, in much less of a hurry, lingered too long, and got a fatal dose. The evident truth of this helped our client set aside a measure of her guilt, I am happy to report, and allowed her to begin grieving properly.

The First Curiosity

Upon reflection, no, it is in fact a wild bilking. Two 6" circles together are half as large as one 12" circle. Mrs. Hudson should have paid half her usual sum.

The Cult of the Red Star

It turns out he was referring to the same man by each of those relationships. The victim's mother was the murderer's sister (father's brother-in-law). The victim had a brother, who had married the murderer's daughter (brother's father-in-law), and he himself had married the daughter of the murderer's brother (father-in-law's brother).

Afternoon

It can only be twenty-six minutes to six.

Dimples

"They contribute in two ways," Holmes informed me. "First, by making the surface of the ball irregular, they help trap the air that they fly through for longer. This reduces the wake that the ball leaves in the air, which in turn reduces the drag on it. Less drag, less deceleration, and the ball flies further. The other is due to the spin of the ball. Golf clubs impart backspin to the ball, and thanks to that backwards spin, the flow lines of the air around the ball are pushed downwards, effectively pushing the ball upwards, and greatly lengthening its distance. Without dimples, the air will tend to just scoot straight over the ball without being pushed."

SUFFOCATION

The question that Holmes asked was: "Did you see the time reflected in the hall mirror?" The poor maid gasped, and went as white as a sheet, because of course that was exactly what she had done. The nephew had left at 6:11, not at 5:49, and eventually the murderous fool confessed that he'd killed his aunt in desperation, as she was about to write him out of her will.

THE FIRST LITERAL ODDITY

They are all words which have no repeated letters. Being fifteen letters long, they each make use of more than half of the alphabet. I was amused to note that despite this, there are six letters which none of the four encompasses.

The First Mental Trial

The four are descended from each other in a straight line. It is the only way to order the switching around. George is Alfie's father, Fred is Alfie's son, and Harry is Alfie's infant grandson.

Watch Out

"It's the difference in air pressure," Holmes informed me. "Higher up, the air is thinner. Makes it harder to breathe, but it also means that the air gives less resistance to the watch spring. This makes it run faster."

Afghan Shot

Along one short side of the box, you can fit 85 balls, placed as 13 rows alternating 7 and 6 balls. The next layer above can fit twelve rows, again alternating, to give 78 balls. This pattern of layers can be repeated all along the length, to a total of 15 layers. Summing these up, 8 layers of 85 balls and 7 layers of 78 gives us a full crate of 1,226 balls.

The Dinner Table

There is only one pair of solutions that will give each man new partners every time, and yet still keep George 3 seats away around the table, and Bill just two seats distant. These are as follows: Alfie, Fred, Bill, Don, George, Eric, Charlie; and Alfie, Eric, Bill, George, Charlie, Fred, Don.

The Bicycle

If you process through the years and consider the ratios, the answer will quickly become apparent. Three times 13 is 39, seven years out; a year later, three times 14 is 42, five years off the mother's new age of 47. So for each year that passes, the time to close the gap shortens by two years. If you stick with jumping whole years however, the gap will go from 1 year to -1 year, so you need to use a half-year to get the gap to exactly zero. At 15, it is 3 years difference, at 16 it is 1 year, so at 16½ the girl will be exactly a third of her mother's age, which will be 49½. The girl has to wait 3½ years.

Highland Fling

"It's as plain as the hairs on your head, Watson. The supposed witch packed the bell with snow before her dramatic entrance. It stopped the bell sounding, and then either shook loose thanks to the exertions of the bell-ringer, or melted away in the intervening time. I'd need to check in person to see which, and I have no intention of doing any such thing. Either way, the addled locals failed to notice the obvious explanation, turning instead to the most arrant foolishness."

Big Squares

You will discover that the smallest possible nine-digit square number which makes use of each of the digits once and once alone is 139,854,276.

The Second Literal Oddity

To my surprise, it turns out that there are just three words ending in -bt, doubt, debt and redoubt. Their commonality fooled me into the assumption that if I could think of three off the top of my head there had to be many more, but it is not the case. Likewise, there are just three standard words ending with -gry – angry, hungry, and the reasonably obscure puggry, the latter being a light head-scarf worn over a hat as additional solar protection.

The Switch

It is an interesting fact that the number of pairs of times when the hands of a clock switch exact position can be calculated from the hour as such: consider how many whole hours there are from the current hour to midnight, and subtract one. The current hour is 3, so there nine hours to midnight, and our value is eight. Then take your value, and add the whole numbers together, in order, from one, until you reach the same number as your value. If the value was two, you would add 1 and 2, for a total of 3; but ours is 8. Adding these, 1 + 2 + 3 + 4 + 5 + 6 + 7 + 8 gives 36, the correct answer.

The Circus

The murdered performer had taken the magician's assistant as a sweetheart, but he had a lethally jealous rival – the musical conductor. The trapeze act used the musical score to provide the necessary split-second timing. Holmes had heard the conductor change the timing of the music, speeding it up just enough so that when it came to make his dashing leap, the trapeze artist was out of position. He leapt too soon, trusting the music, and crashed to his death.

The First Portmanteau

The solution is that the image points to the Palace of Westminster, commonly referred to as the Houses of Parliament. The elegant building represents the House of Lords, our parliament of inherited peers. The rougher one represents the House of Commons, our elected representatives, although I must hasten to point out that our parliamentarians are to be considered common only in the sense of not being Peers of the Realm. The two Houses are ineluctably intertwined in the government of Britain, as the rope indicates. The arguing men indicate the political divisions in British public life, which ever invite raucous debate – often, I'd wager, such disagreements are more for the look of the thing than from any great variance of principle, but still, disagreements they remain. The pole with the carriage clock represents the mighty St. Stephen's clock tower which so characterises the view of central London. In the image, this is overshadowed by the bell; this reflects the fact that the tower itself is overshadowed by Big Ben – its most famous occupant, the great bell which rings out the hour.

Urchins

Every lad will walk next to every other lad once, so will form eight pairs. Four of those pairs will be formed two at a time, when he is in the middle of the three, and the other four singly, when he is on the end of a group. Therefore he will require six outings to walk with everyone once.

The Meadow of Death

As Holmes pointed out, the lack of any signs of human agency in the couple's demise suggested some sort of environmental factor. We know that they were not poisoned, so toxic gas is ruled out. The lack of broken limbs, the proximity to the village, and their being hand in hand together all suggest that they were not in notable distress prior to their deaths, so that whatever killed them was very sudden. By Holmes' confession, he had made no mention of the length of time that they had been dead. As it transpired, they had been out walking in the winter, and had been completely buried in a sudden slide of snow. They had remained there, hidden, all winter, only to be discovered after the thaw had come.

The Third Literal Oddity

The two are amongst the longest English words which are anagrams of each other. Furthermore, and even more impressively, they do not share any letter-pairs in common, neither is any letter in one of the words in the same position in the other. That is quite a feat, in a fourteen-letter anagram pair.This may be compared to the admittedly longer anagram pair of conservationalists and conversationalists, which at eighteen letters, are the longest non-scientific English anagram pair, but where the only difference is the rather trivial transposition of the 's' and the 'v'.

Gold

The box is 100x100" square, and 11" deep. The floor of the box contains layers of eight by nine slabs, leaving a one inch gap on the side. Eleven of these layers will fill the box to the top, accounting for 792 of the slabs. That leaves eight slabs to go in on their edge in a space 100 inches by 11 inches – one exact row of eight slabs lengthways.

Stones

The distances would rapidly increase to the ludicrous, of course, particularly having to go back and forth each time. In fact, for fifty stones, the distance travelled to collect them all, in yards, would be 50 x 49 x 99 / 3 yards, and 80,850 yards is very nearly 46 miles.

Hudsons Tangled

When Katie was three times as old as Alison, Katie was 16½ and Alison 5½ (11 years younger). Then we get 49½ for the age Alison will be when she is three times as old as Katie was then. When Katie was half this she was 24¾. And at that time Alison must have been 13¾ (11 years younger). Or, in the other direction, Katie is (27½) twice as old as Alison was (13¾) when Katie was half as old (24¾) as Alison will be (49½) when Alison is three times as old (49½) as Katie was (16½) when Katie was (16½) three times as old as Alison (5½).

So the age of Katie to that of Alison must be in the proportion 5 to 3, and as the sum of their ages is 44, Katie is 27½ and Alison 16½.

The Second Curiosity

It took me a long moment to recollect t hat Herod had ordered only boy children slain. All the feet would have belonged to boys.

Fencing

"That sort of tone can only be caused from a flat, dull noise by broken reflections of sound," Holmes explained. "You would need to be near a set of railings of some sort, or something of a similar structure with many small bars close together in parallel. Each one reflects a tiny fraction of the sound, but at a precisely staggered interval, being slightly further away than the last. It is this effect which causes the apparent ringing."

THE SOHO PIT

The man is going twice as deep as he has done so far, so when finished, the hole will be a total of three times its present depth. The current depth of the hole has to be less than his height, and, when finished, greater than his height but less than twice that. Within those bounds, the only solution is that the hole is currently 3ft 6 deep, and when finished, will be 10ft 6.

THE SECOND MENTAL TRIAL

Alfie has two brothers, and four sisters. With three men and four women, each woman has three of each sex of sibling, and each man has two brothers and four sisters. Bill, by comparison, is from a family of five. Each of the brothers has one brother and three sisters, and each of the sisters has two of each. So Alfie, with two brothers, has one more than Bill does.

The Hanged Man

As Holmes was so fond of saying, when the impossible had been discounted, the improbable, no matter how unlikely, had to be the truth. It was impossible that the killer had left the room so securely fastened, so he had to still be in the room, and that meant the death was a suicide. Holmes' fingers were wet after touching the carpet because the artist used a block of ice to stand on when fastening his noose to the ceiling, wearing boots against the cold. Then he kicked the block down flat and died, determined to leave one last riddle. The ice later melted, but the carpet was still damp.

Happy Family

"From what we are told, we know that Barney's age is twice Amelia's, and Charlotte's presence brings their combined total to twice Barney's. This means that together, Amelia and Charlotte combined are worth four times Amelia's age alone, and so Charlotte is three times Amelia's age.

"Later, we are told that Barney and Daniel together total twice Amelia and Charlotte, but Emily's addition reverses this. Again, this tells us that Emily is three times the combined age of Amelia and Charlotte. We know Emily is 21, so Amelia and Charlotte together are 7 years old. Dividing seven into quarters, for Charlotte's age is three times that of Amelia's, we can discern that Amelia is 1¾, whilst Charlotte is 5¼. From here, it is simple. Barney is twice Amelia's age, or 3½, and Daniel's age – by the same logic we used for the girls – has to be three times Barney's, or 10½.

"So Amelia is 1¾, Barney is 3½, Charlotte is 5¼, Daniel is 10½, and Emily, as we know already, is 21 years of age."

The Barn

"I'll put you out of your misery, Inspector. It is a simple enough matter. Your fellow rode to the barn during the snowstorm. The snowfall obliterated the signs of his passing. He then turned the shoes round on his horse, so they were pointing in the wrong direction.

"Without inspecting the barn myself, I cannot say whether he found the tools he needed on site, and was struck by inspiration, or whether he brought them with him with confusion in mind all along. If the latter, he may have removed the horse's shoes before the evening's escapade began. Either way, it is no great matter to put them on back to front.

"Then, with his horse suitably attired, he waited until the snow stopped, and rode off, boldly leaving a clear trail that would be sure to fox his pursuit."

ANSWERS & SOLUTIONS

"It is a capital mistake to theorize before one has data. Insensibly one begins to twist facts to suit theories, instead of theories to suit facts."

Sherlock Holmes

The Third Mental Trial

It might be tempting to divide the money up according to the amount of oil each man had before the operation, 8 and 5 farthings, but that would be unfair to Alfie. Thirteen pints of oil are split between the three men. That leaves each man with 4 and 1/3 pints. Bill has lost just 2/3 of a pint of oil; the bulk of the donation has come from Alfie, who has lost 3 and 2/3.

To discover a fair breakdown, first think of the entire donation in terms of thirds of a pint. 3 pints is 9 third-pints, as any publican will tell you, so Alfie has lost 11 thirds to Bill's 2. The fair division of the money then is 11 farthings to Alfie, and 2 to Bill.

In Paris

As Holmes eventually pointed out, the only two rational possibilities were either that the woman was demented, or that the entire hotel staff were colluding against her. The former option, whilst neat, would hardly have occasioned his presenting the matter to me in such a manner.

As it happened, the staff were indeed colluding. The brother had been diagnosed with severe typhoid fever during the night, and was immediately whisked away to a small, quiet hospice outside the city. Terrified that news of the lethally infectious disease might panic the World's Fair visitors and lead to a scandalous financial disaster, the manager had the room sealed and disguised, and briefed all the staff to remain resolute in the face of the lady's questioning.

Pop Pop

"It is a matter of air pressure," said Holmes. "The heat of the boiler turns the water inside it to steam. Steam takes up much more space that water does, so the pressure of this steam bubble forces the water in the bottom of the exhaust to be expelled in a jet. The boat is pushed forwards by the force of this jet. The relative coolness of the exhaust pipe – compared to the boiler – almost immediately causes the steam bubble to condense back into water. This creates an empty vacuum, because the mechanism is closed off from the air, and the water is sucked back up the exhaust to its position prior to the beginning of the expansion. It is then heated back to steam, and the cycle repeats."

"That's all well and good," I replied, "but why doesn't the second part of the operation cancel out the first?"

"Ah, that's the clever bit. When the water is expelled, it is pushed out in one direction alone, all its force concentrated, so the boat accelerates off in the other direction. But when it is drawn back in, it comes in from all around the end of the pipe, in every direction, so the force is all spread out, and the boat cannot react against it. If you wish a demonstration, trying to extinguish a candle flame by sucking air rather than blowing it. Do mind not to burn your lips, however!"

Evasion

The simplest approach is to round up the combined age a little, to 50. Then it can be seen fairly easily that if the man is 30 and the woman 20, when he was 20, she would have been 10, and he would have been twice her age.

The real sum is not quite so neat, but now we know the approximate divisions, it is reasonably straightforward to ascertain that he is twenty-nine and two fifths, and she is nineteen and three-fifths. When he was the latter age, she was half that, at nine and four fifths.

Six-Sided Dice

Consider 1 die first of all. The 4, 5 and 6 can be discounted, as their positions are fixed by the earlier numbers. Then the 1 can be marked on any of 6 faces. That leaves 4 faces for the 2 to occupy, and 2 faces for the three. Multiplying these out, there are 48 options for marking one die. Each subsequent die can be marked independently of the other two, so the grand total of possible marking schemes for three six-sided dice is 110,592.

The Fourth Mental Trial

I must admit that I was unable to find an answer until Holmes suggests that I write the words down using only capital letters, to wit CHECKBOOK and EXCEEDED. Then it became clear that they were composed entirely of letters that possessed horizontal symmetry as capitals. If you placed a mirror over the top half of the word and reflected the bottom half with it, it would be unchanged. I dare say you could contrive the word 'COOKBOOKED', or some similar chimera, but I personally feel that would be something of a dodge.

The Dictionary

With care, it proved possible to arrange the books so that the fifth protruded entirely over the table. The trick lies in counting back from the top book. It is possible to push one single book up to half-way out without having it topple. To then extend the second book over a third, one can go just half the distance of the one above. To extend that third, half as much again, and so on. Proceeding in this manner, after extending the fifth book, the top volume is just a little clear of the base.

Holmes assured me that there was no theoretical maximum as to how far clear the top book may be extended. I politely informed him that I believed him implicitly, and would be happy to watch if he was minded to provide a demonstration, but that I was not inclined to physically test the maxim any further. No such demonstration has yet been forthcoming.

The Third Curiosity

I was astounded to hear that it would raise the girdle by very nearly a full yard – approximately 19/20ths, if you wish to be more precise.

The Fish Murder

"What blade could a man leave behind in an enemy's neck, yet have it vanish into thin air within minutes, Watson?"

I had to confess my bafflement.

"Ice, dear fellow. A spike of ice. Easily prepared and brought in with the ice packing the day's catch. It would stay strong enough to create a piercing wound for several minutes, but would be completely gone in short order, particularly if left within the heat of flesh. Weir was unlucky with the timing of the patrol, but by running, ensured the constables were distracted long enough for the blade to melt away."

A Hearty Drop

The first action is to fill the pail, and then fill the jar from the pail. Alfie then quaffs the contents of the pail. There are now 7 pints in the barrel, 3 pints in the jar, and 2 pints in Alfie.

Next, the contents of the jar are poured back into the pail, and the jar is filled again from the barrel. That leaves 4 pints in the barrel, which Bill grabs happily, and three pints in each vessel.

The jar is poured into the pail until the pail is full, leaving 1 pint inside the jar, and five in the pail. Charlie drinks the pint in the jar. Then the jar is filled again from the pail, leaving two pints inside it. Charlie takes the jar, for his four pints in total, and Alfie gets the pail, with his remaining two pints. The men can then take more time over their remaining drinks, although Bill has some catching up to do.

The Box

From the extension of Pythagoras' theorem, it can be seen that the areas of the top and side multiplied together and then divided by the area of the end give the square of the length. 120 x 96 / 80 gives us 144, so the box is 12 inches in length. From there, it is simple to see that it is 10 inches broad, and 8 inches deep.

Sheep

"At no point did I tell you that the pens had to be empty before you began, Watson. If one of the pens contains a sheep already, the matter is trivial. I do not present this problem to make sport with you, but to highlight that it is vital to look for solutions which are beyond the obvious."

The Second Portmanteau

As I eventually managed to deduce, the image refers to Hyde Park. The river Serpentine is the dominant feature of the park, hence the coils of water ending in the head of a snake. The park was the site of the first World's Fair in 1851, the Great Exhibition, which was housed in the great Crystal Palace, which was later rebuilt, in modified form, in Penge. The park is also host to Speaker's Corner, where by tradition any man or woman may go to freely speak his mind, represented by the wild-tempered fellow on the box. It is perhaps an irony that Speaker's Corner is just a few yards away from the site of the infamous Tyburn Tree, the three-beamed gallows which took the lives of London's condemned for so many centuries.

Get a Hat

It should be clear that one person with one hat to choose can never be mistaken, two people can get it wrong in just one manner, and three people in just two. In fact, the general rule is that for each increase in the number of people, you need to multiply the previous result by the new total of persons. When that new total of persons is even, you must add 1 to your product, and when it is odd, you must remove one, to make allowance for the fact that an odd number of people have their options slightly restricted.

By calculating through, it will be found that seven men can get the wrong hats in 1,854 different ways. If you wanted to know just the number of all possible different ways the hats could be distributed, that would be 1 x 2 x 3 x 4 x 5 x 6 x 7, or 5,040.

Nephews

"It's quite elementary, my dear fellow. If two men each marry the (possibly widowed) mother of the other, and both father a son upon their new wives, then those sons will be both uncle and nephew to each other, as each will be the brother of the other's father. There are other ways to achieve the relationship too, but that is the most straight-forward."

The Fifth Mental Trial

After I had pondered the matter for a while, Holmes came to my rescue. "You can do it in just two operations," he assured me. "Divide the coins into three piles of three. Place two upon the scales and compare them. If one side is lighter, that pile contains the fake; if the two are equal, the set-aside pile holds it. Clear the scale, and take the pile with the fake. Now place any two of the coins upon the scales and again compare. If one is lighter, it is the fake; if they are the same, it is the held-over coin. The method is infallible."

Equity

The solution which most readily presents itself to me is this:

79 + 5 + 1/3 = 84 + 2/6

I do not believe that it can be done without the use of fractions.

Twenty Thousand Leagues

"It's a matter of buoyancy, old friend. While the device remained surrounded by water on all sides, the pressure of that water would be pushing in all directions, including upwards. Therefore it would not present too great an impediment to progress. So long as it did not crush the submersible like an egg, anyway. However, if the machine was allowed to land, this could drive the water out from underneath the device. Suddenly there would be no upward pressure, just downwards. Lacking the most incredible engines, the machine would be pinned in place, like a butterfly in a case – a death sentence to be sure."

The Shoreditch Bank

The reason for the apparent lapse in security was clearly obvious as soon as we entered the office. The clever villains had prepared an accurate depiction of the safe, somewhat larger than the real thing, and propped it up so as to appear, from the door, as if nothing was wrong. They were then able to work on opening the safe, and when the guards came past and looked in, everything appeared to be in order. The deception would have been more obvious if the office had been brightly lit, but as it was, it was more than sufficient to buy the thieves the time they needed. Even Holmes seemed a little impressed by their ingenuity.

Markham

"There are two lines of approach to solving this problem. One is the elliptical. You may notice, on the side table, a bottle of pills near to the decanter of Scotch. Markham was ill, and as the widow did not mention it, we can assume she did not know. Furthermore, it bespeaks a certain bleakness of outlook when a man keeps his medication next to his hard liquor.

"The other approach is more direct. The room was sealed from the inside, and we are told it is impossible that the intruder escaped unseen. It is within reason that both widow and maid may be in cahoots, but if they allowed an assailant to escape, how did they seal the room back up without being caught within it?

"No Watson, the matter is far more straightforward. If it is impossible that anyone escaped, then the unlikely must be true, and the killer is still in there – dead. Markham's prognosis must have been stark enough that he could not bear to suffer through it. He locked the room, staged the argument, and took his own life. If you look through his paperwork, I have no doubt you'll find a life insurance policy that pays handsomely in case of murder, but not at all when it comes to suicide. Let the police seek their unlikely suspect however. I see no need to burden the widow any further."

Montenegro

The suitable pairs would be 5 and 9 for one player, and 13 and 15 for the other. You can make 5 in six ways, and 9 in twenty-five, for a total of 31 chances; and you can make 13 in 21 ways, and 15 in 10 ways, also for 31 chances. In any given throw with these numbers, there will be a 1/7th chance of attaining victory.

Wordplay

Given that there are no English words without a vowel – Y is not in our range of options, remember – then our possible maximum number of words is restricted to the groups that contain one of these four. A further restriction is that there is no common English word formed from just three vowels. Even if we had a U available, I.O.U. is an abbreviation, not a word. So with that in mind, there are a maximum of 22 non-repetitive groups that contain at least one consonant and at least one vowel. If 'Jek' or its derivatives were words, it would be possible to attain that, but as they are not, the maximum practical is 21:

ALE	FOE	HOD	BGN
CAB	HEN	JOG	KFM
HAG	GEM	MOB	BFH
FAN	KIN	JEK	DFL
JAM	HIM	GCL	LJH
AID	JIB	FCJ	NJD
OAK	FIG	HCK	MLN
BED	OIL	MCD	BLK
ICE	CON		DGK

Wimbledon Common

The cabbie reacted so violently because his passenger gave his own home address as a destination. He had long suspected his wife of being engaged in an illicit affair, so when a perfect stranger asked to be taken to his own home, at a time when he himself ought to be safely out of the way, the man snapped. Instead of taking the visitor to his home, he took him out into the park and slaughtered him. Under French law, it is sometimes permissible for a jealous lover to be treated leniently for murder due to a temporary fit of insanity inflamed by the passions.

The Sixth Mental Trial

"Your sign is white. If any man saw both of the black signs – Bill, let us say – he would know his own had to be white, and he would immediately step forward. Because he does not do so, Alfie can thus be certain that you and he do not between have both the black signs. So far, so good. Now, if you had a black sign, Alfie could be sure that his sign was white, because he knows you are not both wearing black, so he would be able to step forward. However, he does not do so. This can only mean that he sees a white sign on your back as well. Of course, any of the three of you could use parallel logic to arrive at the same conclusion, so it becomes a race of the wits as to which of you gets there first."

Most Irregular

If you try various whole year ages for the lad and work out whether the answers match the conditions, you'll find that you overshoot and undershoot between 9 and 8.

If Wiggins is nine, Father Anthony is 36, and Father Gary is 48. That would make David 16, but nine years ago, four times David's age would have been 28, not Father Anthony's 27, a difference of 1 year too much.

If Wiggins is eight, Father Anthony is 32, and Father Gary is 44. That would make David 14 2/3. Nine years ago, four times David's age would have been 22 2/3, but Father Anthony would have been 23, a difference of 1/3 of a year too little.

The discrepancies are 1/3 one side, and 3/3 the other side – a total of 4/3 of inaccuracy. This means that Wiggin's age lies between 8 and 9 in the same ratio of 1 past 8, and 3 before nine – or 8¼. Father Anthony is 33, and Father Gary is 45. David is 15, and nine years ago would have been 6, whilst Father Anthony was 24; and as 6 times 4 is 24, the ages match.

Carl Black

"Arson is a mark of desperation in an otherwise sober man," Holmes said. "I believe the root cause to be the kidnapping. Black had always been a flamboyant spender, and given the state of the company, it seems likely he had been embezzling. The partner, Robbins, would have needed a lever to move Black with, so I suspect he had discovered the embezzlement. Either way, between them they hatched a kidnap plot, and staged that business with the supposed Serbians. The insurance paid a hefty sum, Black departed quietly – and without scandal. The company finances improved markedly, which I assume was the combined benefit of the end of the embezzlement and the surreptitious slow feeding back in of the ransom money. All was well until Black got himself killed. Robbins felt that he couldn't take the risk that Black might have retained some sort of incriminatory document regarding the kidnapping amongst his effects, and panicked. It will all come out as the arson trial proceeds, mark my words."

A Matter of Time

"The trick, dear fellow, is to make sure the two sticks are not touching, and light both ends of one, and just one end of the other. The stick burning from both ends will burn out in 30 minutes, whilst the second stick is still half-way through. At that point, light the other end of the second stick, and it will burn out in 15 minutes, for a total of 45 minutes."

THE FAULTY WATCH

It is a curious fact that the hands of a clock meet in their regular journey exactly every $65\frac{5}{11}$ minutes. So if my watch hands are meeting every 64 minutes, my watch is fast, and is gaining almost one and a half minutes every hour.

A PUZZLING PORTMANTEAU

A pretty riddle, this one. It was the trees and plants that first set me on the right track. They are all different, and arranged with precision. Where would you find a wide variety of both trees and plants, precisely arranged? The most obvious answer would be to look in a herbarium. With that decided, it was only a matter of time before my mind turned to the Royal Botanic Gardens at Kew, and all the pieces fell into place.

Occupying 120 hectares of gardens and glasshouses, Kew Gardens holds the largest herbarium on Earth, as well as a vast collection of living specimens. Their habitats include the impressive Palm House and Temperate House, respectively the first and largest wrought-iron glass-houses in existence. The former's beguiling curves are hinted at in the glass-house shown picture, as is the scale of the latter. The Alpine House provides a cold environment for chill-weather plants. The Great Pagoda is one of the Gardens' more impressive follies, and for some time was the largest Chinese-style building in Europe.

The last piece of the puzzle is the 'farmer King' – King George III, God rest his soul. 'Farmer George' was a passionate agriculturalist, and he carried out several trials and adjustments at Kew. This even included a brave plan to strengthen British sheep by crossbreeding them with stolen specimens from Spain's famous, and well guarded, Merino flocks.

The Ladies of Morden

To get an answer which works effectively, you have to go through the players cyclically. Once that is understood, it becomes a matter of finding suitable starting places for each column at the beginning, and descending from there.

1.	A B vs I L	E J vs G K	F H vs C D
2.	A C vs J B	F K vs H L	G I vs D E
3.	A D vs K C	G L vs I B	H J vs E F
4.	A E vs L D	H B vs J C	I K vs F G
5.	A F vs B E	I C vs K D	J L vs G H
6.	A G vs C F	J D vs L E	K B vs H I
7.	A H vs D G	K E vs B F	L C vs I J
8.	A I vs E H	L F vs C G	B D vs J K
9.	A J vs F I	B G vs D H	C E vs K L
10.	A K vs G J	C H vs E I	D F vs L B
11.	A L vs H K	D I vs F J	E G vs B C

A Fascinating Curiosity

Although the effect is vanishingly small for a billiard table, to remain perfectly level for the players, it would have to follow the curvature of the Earth. If it were perfectly level, it would be closest to the Earth at its centre point, and the balls would all roll to the middle.

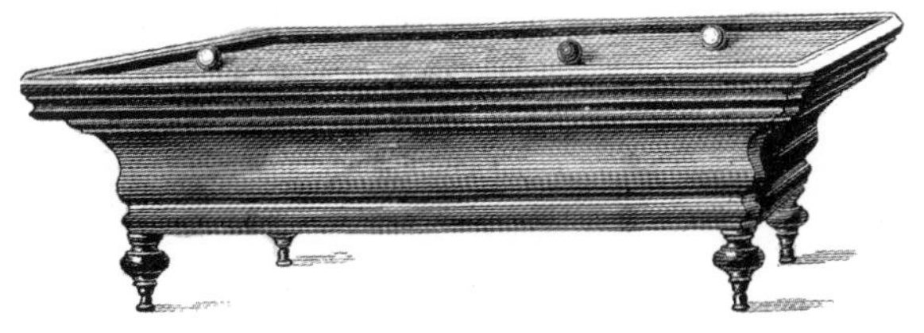

Groups

There are in fact two solutions to the problem. These are: 4 x 1,738 = 6,952 and 4 x 1,963 = 7,852. In both cases, all nine digits are used just once.

The Eggtimer's Companion

There are only two sets of four numbers totalling 100 which have the squares of their lesser three numbers summing equal to the square of the larger. Thus Mr. Southwell is 39, his wife 34, his daughter 14, and his son 13, whilst Mr. Adams is 42, his wife 40, his daughter 10 and his son 8.

A Curious Mental Trial

The answer is 17. As I finally realised, the numbers are in increasing length when spelled out fully as words. Two has 3 letters, five has 4, and so on, up to fourteen with eight digits. The only number with nine digits that is less than twenty is seventeen.

Cones

"It is a general rule in this instance," Holmes later informed me, "that the greatest volume may be produced by cutting at just one third of the maximum height."

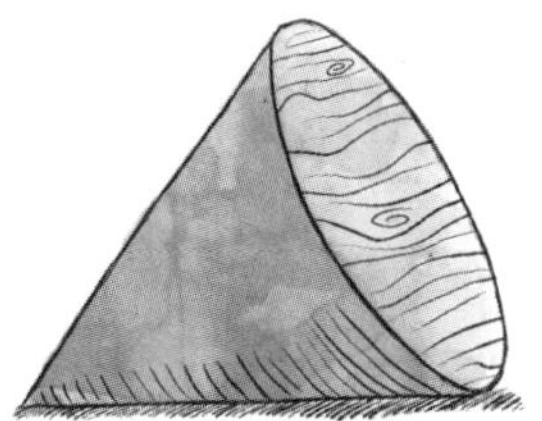

Down on the Farm

The injuries were consistent with a fall from a significant height, and as Holmes pointed out, this would be consistent with the lack of any trail or drag-marks near the body's original site. The peculiarly heavy clothing further suggested that the man would have expected to be in cooler air. Together, Holmes took this to mean that he fell from an aeronautic balloon. This mode of transport would suit a spy who wished to depart from England's shores without the risk of alerting any authorities.

The clincher, for Holmes, was the half-match. He suggested that a group of spies had been attempting to escape the country, possibly in advance of an impending arrest. Taking to a Montgolfier balloon, they were above West Sussex when it became obvious that they had to lighten their load beyond the capacity of ballast to correct, or else risk being grounded and captured. They drew lots, and the unfortunate wretch before us happened to obtain the shortened matchstick. Rather than endanger the mission, he emptied his pockets and leapt to his death.

BOARD

As it turns out, the number of rectangles (including squares) enclosed by such a square board of squares is equal to the (mathematical) square of the triangular order equal to the number of (physical) squares on the board.

In this case, the board is 8 units long. The 8th triangular number is 36 – 1+2+3+4+5+6+7+8. Square 36, and you'll arrive at the correct answer, 1,296. The formula for deriving the exact number of these which are squares is slightly more complex, but if you are curious, 204 are squares and 1092 are non-square rectangles.

The Night Watchman

As the hands meet every 65 and 5/11 minutes, there are eleven occasions in twelve hours where the hands are together. The hands are together exactly at twelve o'clock, of course. So the first occasion after that when the hands coincide is 1.05 and 27 3/11th seconds. Keep adding the sum, and you will discover only one occasion when the second hand would be near 49 – that is at 4.21 and 49 1/11th seconds. So that was the time of the robbery.

A Literal Oddity

It took me a long time, but I did finally manage to find Holmes' word – sestettes. These are the second divisions of Italian-style sonnets, possessing six lines and generally marking the emotional turning point of the poem.

Also Available

Sherlock Holmes' Elementary Puzzles

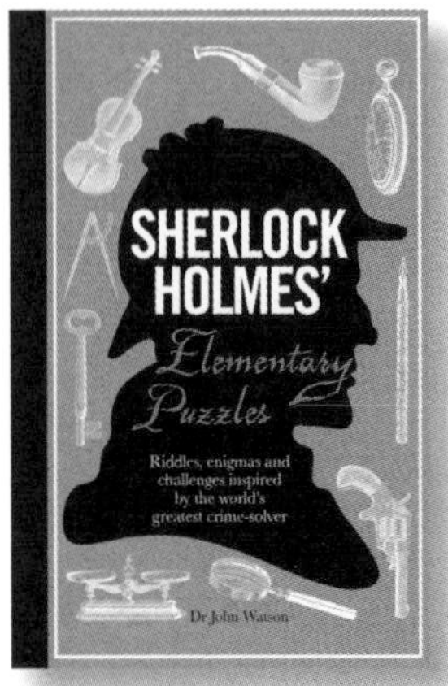

978-1-78097-578-8

Alice's Puzzles in Wonderland

978-1-78097-675-4

The Medieval Puzzle Collection

978-1-78097-577-1